Contents

Cable Throw	2	Bathroom Containers 23
Lavender Bags	5	Bedroom Curtain 26
Fruit Bowl	8	Toy Bag 30
Cushion Cover	10	Nursery Organizer 33
Patchwork Bedcover	13	Draught Excluder 37
Wall Hanger	16	Getting Started 40
		Knitting Techniques 41
		Finishing Touches 45
		Abbreviations 47
Storage Baskets	20	Conversions 48

Introduction

Home is a sanctuary where we relax and escape from the world, where we spend time with family and friends. It is the place that reflects our personalities and our tastes, and provides us with a comforting and comfortable environment to live in. Give your home a makeover with these beautiful knitted projects. The designs reflect the elements that make a home welcoming: the familiar look of handmade things combined with a hint of nostalgia and childhood memories. Snuggle up to warm and soft throws, cheer up a guest room with a new cushion cover or tidy up bathroom bits and bobs with a handy wall hanger.

The designs range from cosy and comforting to bright and fresh. Most of the yarns are pure fibres, making the projects tactile and inviting. A handy techniques section explains all the basic skills needed, so the projects are suitable for beginners and experienced knitters. Whatever your skill level, we're sure you'll find much to inspire.

Cable Throw

Soft, chunky pure wool is used in a warm but neutral colour for this gorgeous throw. The large knotted cable, zigzag with bobbles and four-stitch cable give it a deeply textured feel for warmth and comfort in the living room.

MATERIALS

- Garnstudio Eskimo, 100% wool (54yd/49m per 50g ball): 26 balls in shade 047 Light Beige Mix
- A pair of 9mm (US13:UK00) needles
- 1 x 9mm (US13:UK00) circular needle
- 1 x cable needle

FINISHED SIZE

Approx. 41in (104cm) wide x 41in (104cm) long

TENSION

10 sts and 14 rows to 4in (10cm) over st st using 9mm needles

ALTERNATIVE

This throw is made in panels, so any number and length can be made to vary the size. A cushion cover can also be made by combining panels to form a square and adding a stocking-stitch back.

CABLE PANEL A
(worked over 32 sts)

Row 1: (WS) P2, k6, p6, k4, p6, k6, p2.
Row 2: K2, p6, C6F, p4, C6F, p6, k2.
Row 3: As row 1.
Row 4: K2, p4, (Cr4R, p2, Cr4L) twice, p4, k2.
Row 5: P2, k4, p3, k4, p6, k4, p3, k4, p2.
Row 6: K2, p3, Cr4R, p4, C6B, p4, Cr4L, p3, k2.
Row 7: P2, k3, p3, k5, p6, k5, p3, k3, p2.
Row 8: K2, p2, Cr4R, p5, k6, p5, Cr4L, p2, k2.
Row 9: P2, k2, p3, k6, p6, k6, p3, k2, p2.
Row 10: K2, p2, Cr4L, p5, k6, p5, Cr4R, p2, k2.
Row 11: As row 7.
Row 12: K2, p3, Cr4L, p4, C6B, p4, Cr4R, p3, k2.
Row 13: As row 5.
Row 14: K2, p4, (Cr4L, p2, Cr4R) twice, p4, k2.
Row 15: As row 1.
Row 16: As row 2.
Row 17: As row 1.
Row 18: K2, p6, k3, Cr4L, k2, Cr4R, k3, p6, k2.
Row 19: P2, k6, p3, k2, p6, k2, p3, k6, p2.
Row 20: K2, p6, C5L, C6B, C5R, p6, k2.
Row 21: P2, k8, p12, k8, p2.
Row 22: K2, p8, (C6F) twice, p8, k2.
Row 23: As row 21.
Row 24: K2, p6, Cr5R, C6B, Cr5L, p6, k2.
Row 25: As row 19.
Row 26: K2, p6, k3, Cr5R, Cr5L, k3, p6, k2.
Rows 1 to 26 form cable panel A and are repeated.

CABLE PANEL B
(worked over 36 sts)

Row 1: (WS) P2, k3, p6, k9, p2, k3, p6, k3, p2.
Row 2: K2, p3, k6, p3, Cr3L, p8, k6, p3, k2.
Row 3 and every foll WS row: Knit or purl sts as now set.
Row 4: K2, p3, C6F, p4, Cr3L, p7, C6B, p3, k2.
Row 6: K2, p3, k6, p5, Cr3L, p6, k6, p3, k2.
Row 8: K2, p3, k6, p6, Cr3L, p5, k6, p3, k2.
Row 10: K2, p3, C6F, p7, Cr3L, p4, C6B, p3, k2.
Row 12: K2, p3, k6, p5, MB, p2, Cr3L, p3, k6, p3, k2.
Row 14: K2, p3, k6, p8, Cr3R, p3, k6, p3, k2.
Row 16: K2, p3, C6F, p7, Cr3R, p4, C6B, p3, k2.
Row 18: K2, p3, k6, p6, Cr3R, p5, k6, p3, k2.
Row 20: K2, p3, k6, p5, Cr3R, p6, k6, p3, k2.
Row 22: K2, p3, C6F, p4, Cr3R, p7, C6B, p3, k2.
Row 24: K2, p3, k6, p3, Cr3R, p2, MB, p5, k6, p3, k2.
Rows 1 to 24 form cable panel B and are repeated.

THROW

Centre panel A (make 1)

Using 9mm needles, cast on 32 sts.
Work from panel A until work measures
38½in (98cm), ending with a WS row.
Cast off.

Left side panel A (make 1)

Using 9mm needles, cast on 33 sts.
Row 1: (WS) P3, k6, p6, k4, p6, k6, p2.
Row 2: K2, p6, C6F, p4, C6F, p6, k3.
These 2 rows set the pattern with 3 sts in
st st at LH side.
Work from panel A until work measures
38½in (98cm), ending with a WS row.
Cast off.

Right side panel A (make 1)

Using 9mm needles, cast on 33 sts.
Row 1: (WS) P2, k6, p6, k4, p6, k6, p3.
Row 2: K3, p6, C6F, p4, C6F, p6, k2.
These 2 rows set the pattern with 3 sts in
st st at RH side.
Work from panel A until work measures
38½in (98cm), ending with a WS row.
Cast off.

Centre panel B (make 2)

Using 9mm needles, cast on 36 sts.
Work from panel B until work measures
38½in (98cm), ending with a WS row.
Cast off.

FINISHING OFF

Join panels together.

Top edging

With RS facing, using circular needle, pick
up and knit 116 sts across cast-off edges.
Next row: K to end.
Next row: K1, m1, k to last st, m1, k1.
Rep the last 2 rows once more.
Cast off knitwise.

Bottom edging

With RS facing, using circular needle, pick
up and knit 116 sts across cast-on edges.
Next row: K to end.
Next row: K1, m1, k to last st, m1, k1.
Rep the last 2 rows once more.
Cast off knitwise.

Side edgings

With RS facing, using circular needle, pick
up and knit 116 sts along side edges.
Next row: K to end.
Next row: K1, m1, k to last st, m1, k1.
Rep the last 2 rows once more.
Cast off knitwise.
Join corners.

Lavender Bags

The bamboo- and viscose-mix yarn used for these lavender bags is beautifully soft and silky. One bag has a flower motif taken from the bedcover on page 13, while the other has checks for a traditional look. Both are tied with ribbon and filled with dried lavender.

YOU WILL NEED
- Sublime Bamboo and Pearls DK, 70% bamboo viscose, 30% pearl viscose (104yd/95m per 50g ball)

For the flower bag:
- 1 ball in shade 208 Neroli

For the checked bag:
- 1 ball each of:
  shade 215 Oyster (A)
  shade 208 Neroli (B)

For both bags:
- A pair of size 4mm (US6:UK8) needles
- Dried lavender flowers
- Piece of thin fabric 13 x 6in (33 x 15cm)
- 20in (50cm) length of narrow ribbon (approx. ½in/1cm in width)
- 14in (36cm) length of wider ribbon (approx. 1¼in/2.5cm in width)

FINISHED SIZE
Both bags are 5½in (14cm) wide by 7in (18cm) high

TENSION
22 sts and 28 rows to 4in (10cm) over st st using 4mm needles

FLOWER LAVENDER BAG
Front

Using 4mm needles, cast on 31 sts.
Beg with a purl row, work 8 rows in
rev st st.
Now work flower motif.

Row 1: (RS) P13, k2, p1, k2, p13.
Row 2: K13, p2, k1, p2, k13.
Row 3: P12, k2tog, k1, yrn, p1, yrn, k1, skpo, p12.
Row 4: K12, p3, k1, p3, k12.
Row 5: P11, k2tog, k1, yrn, k1, p1, k1, yrn, k1, skpo, p11.
Row 6: K11, p4, k1, p4, k11.
Row 7: P10, k2tog, k1, yrn, k2, p1, k2, yrn, k1, skpo, p10.
Row 8: K10, p5, k1, p5, k10.
Row 9: P9, k2tog, k1, yrn, k3, p1, k3, yrn, k1, skpo, p9.
Row 10: K9, p6, k1, p6, k9.
Row 11: P8, (k2tog, k1, yf, k1) twice, yf, k1, skpo, k1, yf, k1, skpo, p8.
Row 12: K8, p6, k1, p1, k1, p6, k8.
Row 13: P8, k3, k2tog, k1, yrn, p1, k1, p1, yrn, k1, skpo, k3, p8.

Row 14: K8, p5, k2, p1, k2, p5, k8.
Row 15: P8, k2, k2tog, k1, yrn, p2, k1, p2, yrn, k1, skpo, k2, p8.
Row 16: K8, p4, k3, p1, k3, p4, k8.
Row 17: P8, k1, k2tog, k1, yrn, p3, k1, p3, yrn, k1, skpo, k1, p8.
Row 18: K8, p3, k4, p1, k4, p3, k8.
Row 19: P8, k2tog, k1, yrn, p3, MB, p1, MB, p3, yrn, k1, skpo, p8.
Row 20: K8, p2, k11, p2, k8.
Row 21: P12, MB, p5, MB, p12.
Row 22: K31.
Row 23: P11, MB, p1, (p2tog, yrn) twice, p2, MB, p11.
Row 24: K31.
Row 25: P11, MB, (p2tog, yrn) 3 times, p1, MB, p11.
Row 26: K31.
Row 27: P11, MB, p1, (p2tog, yrn) twice, p2, MB, p11.
Row 28: K31.
Row 29: P12, MB, p5, MB, p12.
Row 30: K31.
Row 31: P14, MB, p1, MB, p14.
This completes the flower motif.
Beg with a knit row, work 8 rows in
rev st st.
Eyelet row: **K2, k2tog, yf, (k6, k2tog, yf) to last 3 sts, k3.
Knit 4 rows.
Next row: K1, skpo, knit to last 3 sts, k2tog, k1 (29 sts).
Picot cast-off row: Cast off 2 sts, (slip remaining st on RH needle back onto LH needle, cast on 2 sts, cast off 4 sts) to end and fasten off remaining st **.

Back

Cast on 31 sts.
Beg with a purl row, work 47 rows in
rev st st.
Work as for front from ** to **.

Finishing off flower bag

Join side seams. Fold over fabric, turn over edges and sew two sides on a sewing machine. Fill with dried lavender flowers. Sew up remaining side. Place inside knitted bag. Thread narrow ribbon through eyelets. Sew wider ribbon to top to form a handle.

CHECK LAVENDER BAG
Back and Front (make 2)

Using 4mm needles and B, cast on 38 sts.
Row 1: K2B, (2A, 2B) to end.
Row 2: P2B, (2A, 2B) to end.
Row 3: K2A, (2B, 2A) to end.
Row 4: P2A, (2B, 2A) to end.
These 4 rows form the pattern.
Work a further 42 rows.
Eyelet row: Using A, k4, k2tog, yf, (k5, k2tog, yf) to last 4 sts, k4.
Using A, knit 3 rows.
Cut off A.
Using B, knit 1 row.
Picot cast-off row: Cast off 2 sts, (slip remaining st on RH needle back onto LH needle, cast on 2 sts, cast off 4 sts) to end and fasten off rem 2 sts.

Finishing off checked bag

Press pieces according to yarn band instructions. Sew pieces together. Sew sides of fabric on sewing machine. Fill with dried lavender flowers. Sew remaining seam. Place inside knitted bag. Thread narrow ribbon through eyelets. Attach wider ribbon to top to form handle.

Fruit Bowl

Space-dyed wool in rich berry tones is used to make this simple garter-stitch bowl. The felting adds an extra firmness to the bowl and gives the colours a soft, blurred look.

MATERIALS

- Noro Kureyon (Aran), 100% wool (110yd/101m per 50g ball): 5 balls in shade 124
- A pair of 6mm (US10:UK4) needles
- 1 x 6mm (US10:UK4) circular needle

FINISHED SIZE

Before felting: approx. 10in (25cm) diameter, 4in (11cm) high
After felting: approx. 8in (20cm) diameter, 3½in (9cm) high

TENSION

14 sts and 20 rows to 4in (10cm) over st st using 6mm needles and with yarn used double before felting

PATTERN NOTES

Yarn is used double throughout. When knitting the base, it may be easier to use the circular needle after about six increase rows to prevent the knitting becoming too tight. Remember to continue to work in rows until all increases have been worked.

FRUIT BOWL

Using 6mm needles, cast on 5 sts.
Next row: Inc in each of next 2 sts, k1, inc in each of next 2 sts (9 sts).
Next and every foll alternate row: K to end.
Row 1: (K1, m1) to last st, k1 (17 sts).
Row 3: (K2, m1) to last st, k1 (25 sts).
Row 5: (K3, m1) to last st, k1 (33 sts).
Row 7: (K4, m1) to last st, k1 (41 sts).
Cont in this way, increasing 8 sts on 10 foll RS rows (121 sts).
Change to circular needle.
Next row: K to last st on LH needle. Place a marker here to indicate end of rounds, k last st tog with next st on LH needle (120 sts).
Work in rounds as follows:
Round 1: P to end to form edge of base.
Round 2: K to end.
Rounds 3–9: Repeat rounds 1 and 2 three times, and round 1 again.
Round 10: K15, (m1, k30) 3 times, m1, k15 (124 sts).
Rounds 11–23: Repeat rounds 1 and 2 six times, and round 1 again.
Round 24: K16, (m1, k31) 3 times, m1, k15 (128 sts).
Rounds 25–37: Repeat rounds 1 and 2 six times, and round 1 again.
Round 38: K16, (m1, k32) 3 times, m1, k16 (132 sts).
Rounds 39–47: Repeat rounds 1 and 2 four times, and round 1 again.
Rounds 48–53: K to end.
Cast off loosely.

FINISHING OFF

With WS facing, gather round cast-on sts and pull up tightly. Join base seam. Felt the bowl by following the instructions given on page 44.

ALTERNATIVE

This bowl can be made to any size. You could try using solid colours, or higher sides for storage in other rooms.

Cushion Cover

Soft merino yarns in coffee and cream are used for this tactile cushion cover. Deeply textured rosettes sit upon a simple intarsia circle motif.

MATERIALS
- Debbie Bliss Rialto Aran, 100% wool (88yd/80m per 50g ball):
  3 balls in shade 25 Coffee (A)
  3 balls in shade 01 Stone (B)
  2 balls in shade 16 Cream (C)
- A pair each of 4.5mm (US7:UK7) and 5mm (US8:UK6) needles
- 18 x 18in (45 x 45cm) cushion pad

FINISHED SIZE
Approx. 18 x 18in (45 x 45cm)

TENSION
18 sts and 24 rows to 4in (10cm) over st st using 5mm needles

PATTERN NOTES
When working from the chart, right-side rows are knit rows and read from right to left. Wrong-side rows are purl rows and read from left to right. Use separate balls of yarn for each area of colour and twist yarn on wrong side to avoid a hole when changing colour.

CUSHION COVER
Knitted in one piece starting at top back.

Back
Using 4.5mm needles and A, cast on 81 sts.
Moss st row 1: K1, (p1, k1) to end.
This row forms the moss st.
Work 5 more rows.
Change to 5mm needles.
Beg with a knit row, work 80 rows in st st. Mark each end of last row with a coloured thread.

Front
Work a further 20 rows in st st.
Work in pattern from chart.
Row 1: K15A, pattern across 51 sts of row 1 of chart, k15A.
Row 2: P15A, pattern across 51 sts of row 2 of chart, p15A.
These 2 rows set the position of the chart.
Keeping 15 sts in A at each side, continue to follow chart until 66 rows have been worked.
Continue in A only.
Work a further 20 rows in st st.
Place a marker at each end of last row.

Overlap and buttonhole band
Work a further 22 rows in st st.
Change to 4.5mm needles.
Work 2 rows in moss st.
Buttonhole row: Moss st 7, (work 2tog, yrn, moss st 14) 4 times, work 2tog, yrn, moss st 8.
Work 3 rows in moss st.
Cast off in moss st.

ROSETTES
(make 8)
Using 4.5mm needles and C, cast on 113 sts.
Row 1: K1, (k2, pass first st over 2nd st) to end (57 sts).
Row 2: P to end.
Row 3: K1, (k2 tog) to end (29 sts).
Row 4: P1, (p2tog) to end (15 sts).
Row 5: As row 3 (8 sts).
Break off yarn, leaving a piece approx. 10in (25cm) long. Draw through remaining sts and fasten off tightly, but do not break off yarn (this can be used to attach to cushion cover).

FINISHING OFF
Pin one rosette at centre of circle motif, and secure. Pin the rest of the rosettes closely around the first one, and secure. Using coloured threads to denote fold line, sew side seams. Sew on buttons.

ALTERNATIVES
The cushion cover could be just a simple circle with no rosettes, or the rosettes could be placed in different positions. Try pink and lilac for a feminine look, or one colour for a simple design. The flowers can be used on other projects, too.

ROSETTE CUSHION COVER CHART
(51 sts x 66 rows)

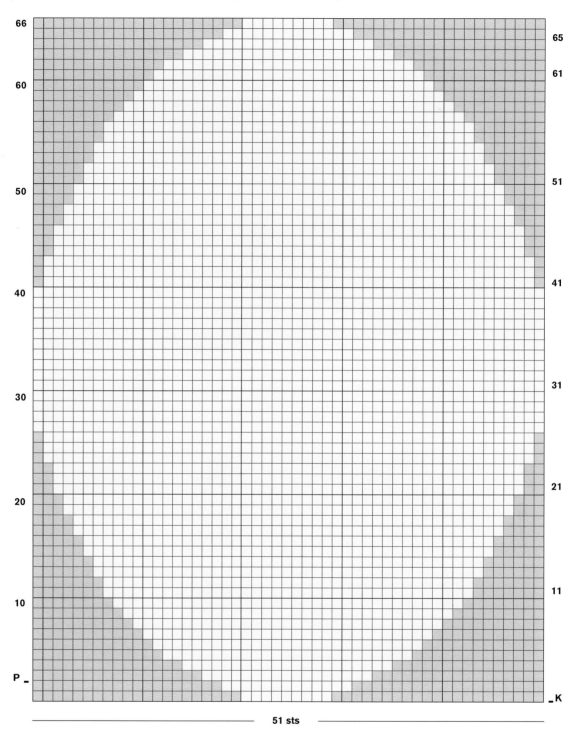

51 sts

Key to chart

A shade 25
B shade 01

1 square represents 1 stitch and 1 row

Patchwork Bedcover

Eco yarn is used in classic cream for this
pretty patchwork bedcover. Tactile bobbles, eyelets
and bobble flowers create a comforting traditional cover
to make your guests feel warm and welcome.

MATERIALS
- Sirdar Eco DK 100% Undyed
  Virgin Wool (109yd/100m per
  50g ball):
  24 balls in shade 200 Ecru
- A pair of 4mm (UK8:US6) needles
- 1 x 4mm (UK8:US6) circular
  needle

FINISHED SIZE
Approx. 53in (134cm) wide x 34in
(87cm) long

TENSION
22 sts and 28 rows to 4in (10cm)
over st st using 4mm needles

ALTERNATIVES
As this is made in squares, any
number can be knitted for different
sizes. Try bright colours for a child's
room, or neutrals for a throw in a
lounge. A cushion cover could be
made with four squares.

LARGE FLOWER MOTIF
(make 30)

Leaving a 12in (30cm) end of yarn for sewing up, cast on 31 sts. Beg with a purl row, work 8 rows in rev st st.
Now work flower.
Row 1: (RS) P13, k2, p1, k2, p13.
Row 2: K13, p2, k1, p2, k13.
Row 3: P12, k2tog, k1, yrn, p1, yrn, k1, skpo, p12.
Row 4: K12, p3, k1, p3, k12.
Row 5: P11, k2tog, k1, yrn, k1, p1, k1, yrn, k1, skpo, p11.
Row 6: K11, p4, k1, p4, k11.
Row 7: P10, k2tog, k1, yrn, k2, p1, k2, yrn, k1, skpo, p10.
Row 8: K10, p5, k1, p5, k10.
Row 9: P9, k2tog, k1, yrn, k3, p1, k3, yrn, k1, skpo, p9.
Row 10: K9, p6, k1, p6, k9.
Row 11: P8, (k2tog, k1, yf, k1) twice, yf, k1, skpo, k1, yf, k1, skpo, p8.
Row 12: K8, p6, k1, p1, k1, p6, k8.
Row 13: P8, k3, k2tog, k1, yrn, p1, k1, p1, yrn, k1, skpo, k3, p8.
Row 14: K8, p5, k2, p1, k2, p5, k8.
Row 15: P8, k2, k2tog, k1, yrn, p2, k1, p2, yrn, k1, skpo, k2, p8.
Row 16: K8, p4, k3, p1, k3, p4, k8.
Row 17: P8, k1, k2tog, k1, yrn, p3, k1, p3, yrn, k1, skpo, k1, p8.
Row 18: K8, p3, k4, p1, k4, p3, k8.
Row 19: P8, k2tog, k1, yrn, p3, MB, p1, MB, p3, yrn, k1, skpo, p8.
Row 20: K8, p2, k11, p2, k8.
Row 21: P12, MB, p5, MB, p12.
Row 22: K31.
Row 23: P11, MB, p1, (p2tog, yrn) twice, p2, MB, p11.
Row 24: K31.
Row 25: P11, MB, (p2tog, yrn) 3 times, p1, MB, p11.
Row 26: K31.
Row 27: P11, MB, p1, (p2tog, yrn) twice, p2, MB, p11.
Row 28: K31.
Row 29: P12, MB, p5, MB, p12.
Row 30: K31.
Row 31: P14, MB, p1, MB, p14.
This completes the flower motif. Beg with a knit row, work 9 rows rev st st. Cast off, leaving a 12in (30cm) end for sewing up.

SMALL FLOWER MOTIF
(make 30)

Leaving a 12in (30cm) end of yarn for sewing up, cast on 31 sts.
Row 1: (RS) K to end.
Row 2 and every WS row: P to end.
Row 3: K5, (yf, skpo, k8) twice, yf, skpo, k4.
Row 5: K3, (k2tog, yf, k1, yf, skpo, k5) twice, k2tog, yf, k1, yf, skpo, k3.
Row 7: K5, (MK, k9) twice, MK, k5.
Rows 9 and 11: K to end.
Row 13: K10, yf, skpo, k8, yf, skpo, k9.
Row 15: K8, k2tog, yf, k1, yf, skpo, k5, k2tog, yf, k1, yf, skpo, k8.
Row 17: K10, MK, k9, MK, k10.
Row 19: K to end.
Row 20: P to end.
Rows 21–48: Rep rows 1 to 20 once, then rows 1 to 8 again.
Cast off, leaving a 12in (30cm) end of yarn for sewing up.

TOP EDGING

Join motifs together to form a rectangle 10 motifs wide by 6 motifs deep.
With RS facing, using circular needle, pick up and knit 290 sts along cast-off edges.
Next row: K to end.

Next row: K1, m1, k to last st, m1, k1.
Rep the last 2 rows twice more (296 sts).
Cast-off row: Cast off 4 sts, (cast on 2 sts, cast off 6 sts) to end.

BOTTOM EDGING

With RS facing, using circular needle, pick up and knit 290 sts along cast-on edges.
Next row: K to end.
Next row: K1, m1, k to last st, m1, k1.
Rep the last 2 rows twice more (296 sts).
Cast-off row: Cast off 4 sts, (cast on 2 sts, cast off 6 sts) to end.

SIDE EDGINGS
(alike)

With RS facing, using circular needle, pick up and knit 178 sts along side edges.
Next row: K to end.
Next row: K1, m1, k to last st, m1, k1.
Rep the last 2 rows twice more (184 sts).
Cast-off row: Cast off 4 sts, (cast on 2 sts, cast off 6 sts) to end.

FINISHING OFF

Join corners.

Wall Hanger

Stripes, fish and starfish create a seaside theme in jaunty nautical colours. Practical cotton Aran is used for this handy pocket storage in which to tidy away all your bathroom bits and pieces.

YOU WILL NEED
• Rico Creative Cotton Aran, 100% cotton (93yd/85m per 50g ball):
3 balls in shade 38 Dark Blue (A)
2 balls in shade 60 Natural (B)
1 ball in shade 41 Pistachio (C)
• A pair of 4.5mm (US7:UK7) needles
• 2 pieces dowelling, 18in (45cm) long

FINISHED SIZE
18in (45cm) wide x 18in (45cm) high

TENSION
18 sts and 24 rows to 4in (10cm) over st st using 4.5mm needles

PATTERN NOTES
When working from a chart, right-side rows are knit rows and read from right to left. Wrong-side rows are purl rows and read from left to right. Use separate balls of yarn for each area of colour and twist yarn on wrong side to avoid a hole when changing colour.

BASE
Using 4.5mm needles and A, cast on 80 sts.
Row 1: K1, p1, k to last 2 sts, p1, k1.
Row 2: K1, p to last st, k1.
These 2 rows form the st st with 2 sts in moss st at each end.
Work a further 8 rows.
Cont in stripe sequence of (2 rows B, 4 rows A) 19 times, 2 rows B, then 10 rows A.
Cast off.

POCKETS
Using 4.5mm needles and A, cast on 22 sts.
Make 5 fish pockets and 4 star pockets, following charts on pages 18–19.
Follow chart to end, working 2 rows moss st at top. Cast off in C.

FINISHING OFF
Press pieces according to yarn band instructions. Place pockets on main piece, pin and sew in place. Turn top and bottom of main piece over to back to form a hem. Cut dowelling to fit the top and bottom and insert.

ALTERNATIVES
You could also make this project in one colour for a bedroom or for kitchen storage.

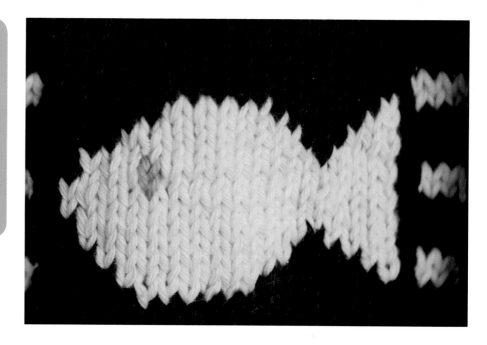

WALL HANGER FISH CHART
(22 sts x 32 rows)

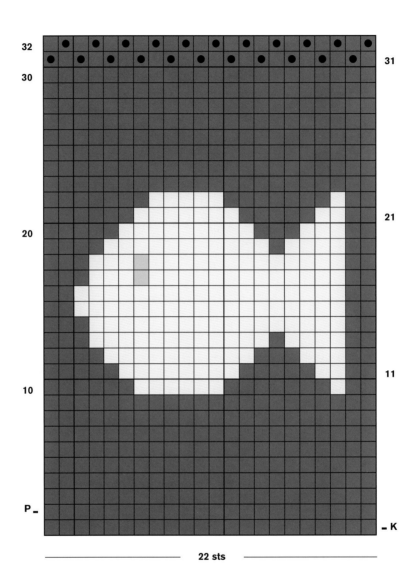

Key to charts

- ■ A shade 38
- □ B shade 60
- ▨ C shade 41

- □ K on RS, P on WS
- ● K on WS, P on RS

1 square represents 1 stitch and 1 row

WALL HANGER STARFISH CHART
(22 sts x 32 rows)

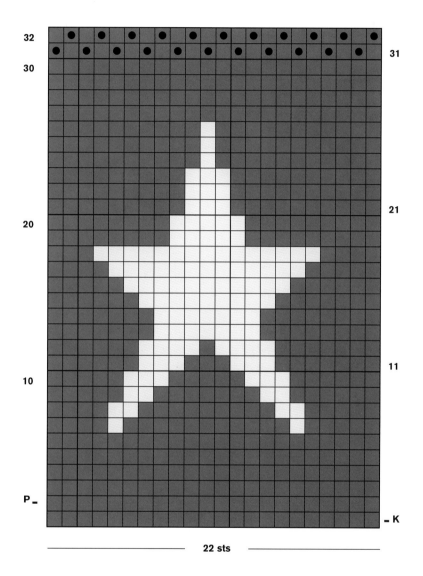

Storage Baskets

A soft, chunky wool in cool wintry colours and a simple double cable is used for these handy containers. Felting makes the knitting firm and adds to the comforting and cosy look.

MATERIALS
- Debbie Bliss Como (chunky), 90% wool, 10% cashmere (46yd/42m per 50g ball):

For the small container:
- 3 balls in shade 06

For the large container:
- 6 balls in shade 05
- A pair of 7.5mm (US11:UK1) needles
- 1 x 7.5mm (US11:UK1) circular needle
- 1 x cable needle

FINISHED SIZE
Before felting (approx.)
Small container: 8in (20cm) diameter, 6in (15cm) high
Large container: 10in (26cm) diameter, 8in (20cm) high
After felting (approx.)
Small container: 5in (13cm) diameter, 4in (10cm) high
Large container: 8in (20cm) diameter, 6in (15cm) high

TENSION
12 sts and 17 rows to 4in (10cm) over st st using 7.5mm needles before felting

CONTAINER

Using 7.5mm needles, cast on 5 sts.

Next row: Inc in each of next 2 sts, k1, inc in each of next 2 sts (9 sts).

Next and every foll alternate row: P to end.

Row 1: (K1, m1) to last st, k1 (17 sts).

Row 3: (K2, m1) to last st, k1 (25 sts).

Row 5: (K3, m1) to last st, k1 (33 sts).

Row 7: (K4, m1) to last st, k1 (41 sts).

Small container only

Cont in this way, increasing 8 sts on 3 foll RS rows (65 sts).

Change to the circular needle.

Next row: (P9, m1) to last 2 sts, p2 (72 sts).

Large container only

Continue in this way increasing 8 sts on 6 foll RS rows (89 sts).

Change to the circular needle.

Next row: (P11, m1) to last st, p this st together with first st on circular needle (96 sts).

Both containers

Cont in rounds to form sides.

Next round: P to end to form edge of base.

Foundation round: P2[3], * inc in each of next 4[6] sts, p4[6]; rep from * to last 6[9] sts, inc in each of next 4[6] sts, p2[3] (108[144] sts).

Rounds 1 and 2: P2[3], * k8[12], p4[6]; rep from * to last 10[15] sts, k8[12], P2[3].

Round 3: P2[3], * C4[6]B, C4[6]F, P4[6]; rep from * to last 10[15] sts, C4[6]B, C4[6]F, p2[3].

Rounds 4–6[8]: Rep rounds 1 and 2 once [twice] and round 1 again.

These 6[8] rounds form the pattern and are repeated throughout.

Work straight until sides are 5[7]in (13[18]cm) from start of sides.

Next round: P to end.

Next round: K to end.

Rep the last 2 rounds once more.

Cast off knitwise.

ALTERNATIVES

These will look good in any room. Try using a 100 per cent wool space-dyed yarn, or leaving the handles off for a different look.

HANDLES
(make 2)

Using 7.5mm needles, cast on 7[10] sts and work in garter st for 6¾[9]in (17[23]cm).

Cast off.

FINISHING OFF

With WS facing, gather round cast-on sts and pull up tightly. Join base seam. Attach handles to inside top at equal distance from each other. Felt the containers by following the instructions given on page 44.

Bathroom Containers

Intarsia fish motifs swim in the waves on a neutral colour base to make these jolly bowl-shaped containers. Knitted in cotton Aran, these useful bathroom accessories are ideal for stashing anything from cotton-wool balls to face cloths.

MATERIALS
- Debbie Bliss Eco Aran Fairtrade Collection, 100% cotton (82yd/75m per 50g ball):

For both bowls
- 3 balls shade 605 (A)
- 1 ball each of shade 622 (B) and shade 601 (C)

Small bowl
- A pair of 4.5mm (US7:UK7) needles

Large bowl
- A pair of 5mm (US8:UK6) needles

FINISHED SIZE
Small bowl: 6in (15cm) diameter, 4in (10cm) high

Large bowl: 8in (20cm) diameter, 6in (15cm) high

TENSION
Small bowl: 18 sts and 24 rows to 4in (10cm) over st st using 4.5mm needles

Large bowl: 16 sts and 22 rows to 4in (10cm) over st st using 5mm needles and yarn double

CONTAINERS

Using 4.5mm needles (for small size), 5mm needles (for large size) and A, cast on 5 sts.

Purl 1 row.

Next row: Inc in each of next 2 sts, k1, inc in each of next 2 sts (9 sts).

Next and every foll WS row:
P to end.

Row 1: K1, (m1, k1) to end (17 sts).
Row 3: K1, (m1, k2) to end (25 sts).
Row 5: K1, (m1, k3) to end (33 sts).
Row 7: K1, (m1, k4) to end (41 sts).
Row 9: K1, (m1, k5) to end (49 sts).
Row 11: K1, (m1, k6) to end (57 sts).
Row 13: K1, (m1, k7) to end (65 sts).
Row 14: K to end.

Sides

Row 15: K to end.
Row 16: P to end.
Row 17: K1, (m1, k8) to end (73 sts).
Row 18: P to end.
Row 19: K1, (m1, k9) to end (81 sts).
Next row: P to end, dec 1 st at centre of row (80 sts).

Work motif as follows in st st:

Row 1: K(8A, 4B) 6 times, 8A.
Row 2: P2B, (4A, 8B) 3 times, 4C (8B, 4A) 3 times, 2B.
Row 3: K(8B, 4A) twice, 7B, 1C, 4A, 1B, 7C, (4A, 8B) 3 times.
Row 4: P2A, (4B, 8A) twice, 4B, 4A, 10C, 3A, 2C, 1A, (4B, 8A) twice, 4B, 2A.

Row 5: K31A, 3C, 1A, 12C, 33A.
Row 6: P32A, 17C, 31A.
Row 7: K31A, 12C, 1A, 3C, 33A.
Row 8: P(8A, 4B) twice, 8A, 2B, 11C, 1B, 3C, 7A, (4B, 8A) twice.
Row 9: K2B, (4A, 8B) twice, 4A, 1B, 2C, 3B, 9C, 5B, (4A, 8B) twice, 4A, 2B.
Row 10: P(8B, 4A) 3 times, 1B, 6C, 1B, 4A, 1C, 7B, (4A, 8B) twice.
Row 11: K2A, (4B, 8A) 3 times, 4C, (8A, 4B) 3 times, 2A.
Row 12: With A only, p to end.

For large bowl only

Work 2 rows st st.

Both sizes

Shape top
Row 1: (K8, k2tog) to end (72 sts).
Rows 2 and 4: P to end.
Row 3: (K7, k2tog) to end (64 sts).
Row 5: (K6, k2tog) to end (56 sts).
Row 6: Knit.

Beg with a knit row, work 8 rows st st.
Cast off.

FINISHING OFF

Join seam.

Bedroom Curtain

Mercerized cotton in a colourful palette is used for this delightful curtain. Butterflies and flowers are attached to long i-cords, to decorate a bedroom window or to make a dramatic entrance to a country garden-inspired room.

MATERIALS
- Patons 100% Cotton DK (230yd/210m per 100g ball):
- 3 balls in shade 692 Cream (A)
- 1 ball each of:
  shade 715 Nougat (B)
  shade 734 Candy (C)
  shade 719 Cheeky (D)
  shade 702 Sky (E)
  shade 701 Lilac (F)
  shade 741 Neroli (G)

Note: This amount is for 8 i-cords, with a mix of flowers and butterflies (51 flowers and 57 butterflies in total). Make more or fewer as required.
- A pair of 2.75mm (US2:UK12) needles
- 2 x 2.75mm (US2:UK12) double-pointed needles
- Piece of dowelling, to fit the width of the doorway or window (this one is ½in/12mm diameter, 31½in/80cm wide)
- Cup hooks to secure dowelling

FINISHED SIZE
Make to fit your window or doorway. Instructions are given for an opening 31in (80cm) wide and 80in (204cm) high.

TENSION
Not critical for this project.

FLOWERS
(make 17 in each colourway)
Colourway 1: F, B, A.
Colourway 2: B, C, A.
Colourway 3: C, F, A.
Using 2.75mm needles and A, cast on 1 st,
k into front, back and front of st (3 sts).
Row 1: P to end.
Row 2: K1, m1, k1, m1, k1 (5 sts).
Row 3: P to end.
Row 4: K to end.
Row 5: P to end.
Row 6: Skpo, k1, k2tog (3 sts).
Row 7: Sl1, p2tog, psso.
Fasten off, leaving a length of yarn.
With RS facing, make a running st around
outer edge and pull tight to form a ball.
Secure, leaving a loose end. These will be
used to sew into centre of flower.

Top petals
(make 5 per flower, worked in garter st)
Using 2.75mm needles and F (B, C), cast
on 3 sts.
Row 1: K1, m1, k1, m1, k1 (5 sts).
Row 2: K to end.
Row 3: K1, m1, k3, m1, k1 (7 sts).

Row 4: As row 2.
Fasten off. Leave sts on the needle being
used. Starting with this needle, make 3
more petals, leaving them on the same
needle, then make one more petal (5 in
total). Do not fasten off.
Next row: K2, sl1, k2tog, psso, k2 across
last petal worked. Rep across the following
4 petals so that there are 5 petals on one
needle (25 sts).
Next row: K1, (k2tog) to end (13 sts).
Rep last row once more (7 sts).
Leave a small length of yarn. Using a
tapestry needle, thread through remaining
sts, pull tight and fasten off.

Outer petals
(worked as one piece)
Using 2.75mm needles and B (C, F), cast
on 9 sts.
Row 1: P to end.
Row 2: K to end.
Row 3: Cast off 6 sts purlwise, p to end.
Row 4: *K to end.
Row 5: Cast on 6 sts, p to end.
Row 6: K to end.
Row 7: As row 3 *.
Rep from * to * 3 times more.
Next row: K to end.
Cast off knitwise, leaving a length of yarn
with RS facing. Join cast-off and cast-on
edges together to form a circle.
Turn petals over to WS facing, thread
length of yarn around inner centre edge,
pull together and secure.

Finishing flowers
Sew bobble to the centre of the top petals,
place lower petals underneath the top
petals, arranging it so that the lower petals
can be seen. Sew in place.
Press petals carefully.

BUTTERFLIES
(make 19 in each colourway)
Colourway 1: G, E, A.
Colourway 2: D, E, A.
Colourway 3: E, D, A.

Top wings
(make two per butterfly)
Work in garter st and short rows.
Using 2.75mm needles and G (D, E),
cast on 7 sts.
Rows 1 and 2: K to end.
Rows 3 and 4: K2, turn, k to end.
Rows 5 and 6: K4, turn, k to end.
Rows 7 and 8: K6, turn, k to end.
Rows 9 and 10: K4, turn, k to end.
Rows 11 and 12: K2, turn, k to end.
Rows 13 and 14: K to end.
Cast off knitwise.

Wing edging
Using 2.75mm needles and E (E, D), with
right side of wing facing, pick up 9 sts
along widest part of the wing edge (outer
edge), turn.
Next row: Cast off knitwise.
Repeat for 2nd wing.

Lower wings
Work in one piece.
Using 2.75mm needles and G (D, E), cast
on 16 sts.
Rows 1 and 2: K to end.
Row 3: K2, skpo, k to last 4 sts, 2tog, k2.
Row 4: K to end.
Rows 5–10: Rep rows 3 and 4 three
times (8 sts).
Row 11: K to end.
Cast off knitwise, leaving a length of yarn.
With this and a tapestry needle, make a
running st through the centre of the lower
wing, pull together to slightly gather the
centre of the wings, secure in place.

Body
Using 2.75mm double-pointed needles and
A, cast on 3 sts.
Row 1: K to end, do not turn work.
Row 2: Slip sts to the other end of the
needle, take yarn across back of work, pull
tightly, k3, do not turn work.

Rep row 2 until i-cord measures 1¾in (4.5cm)
Next row: Sl1, k2tog, psso.
Fasten off.

Finishing butterflies

Sew the top wings together. Slightly overlap the top wings to lower wings, sew in place. Work a French knot (see page 45) in E (E, D) onto the left and right lower corners of the bottom wings. Sew the body onto the centre of the wings. Using a single thread of yarn A, make an antenna, secure and knot each end, cut to neaten ends. Press wings carefully.

I-CORDS
(make 8)

Using 2.75mm double-pointed needles and A, cast on 4 sts.
Row 1: K to end, do not turn work.
Row 2: Slip sts to the other end of the needle, take yarn across back of work, pull tightly, k4, do not turn work.
Rep row 2 until the i-cord measures the correct length for your door frame.

COVER FOR TOP POLE
(make to fit width of doorway or window)

Using 2.75mm double-pointed needles and A, cast on 15 sts.
Beg with a knit row work in st st until work measures 31½in (80cm).
Leaving a long end, cut off yarn and thread through sts.

Fasten tightly, using the yarn to sew the row ends together.
Sew long seam.
Once pole has been put in, sew end with a gathering thread.

FINISHING OFF

Attach butterflies and flowers to the i-cords. Attach i-cords to top pole.

Toy Bag

The Jolly Roger motif on this quirky toy bag warns that pirates are close by! Cotton Aran is used in strong colours and the bag even has a rope-style handle for an added nautical look, making this a fun as well as practical project.

MATERIALS
- Debbie Bliss Eco Aran Fairtrade Collection, 100% cotton (82yd/75m per 50g ball):
- 5 balls in shade 616 (A)
- 1 ball in each of:
  shade 608 (B)
  shade 613 (C)
  shade 618 (D)
- A pair each of 4mm (US6:UK8) and 4.5mm (US7:UK7) needles
- 117in (3m) rope for handle

FINISHED SIZE
17in (44cm) deep x 14in (35cm) wide

TENSION
18 sts and 24 rows to 4in (10cm) over st st using 4.5mm needles

PATTERN NOTES
When working from chart, right-side rows are knit rows and read from right to left. Wrong-side rows are purl rows and read from left to right. Use separate balls of yarn for each area of colour and twist yarn on wrong side to avoid a hole when changing colour.

TOY BAG
Knitted in one piece starting at top back.
Using 4mm needles and A, cast on 65 sts.
Knit 11 rows.
Change to 4.5mm needles.
Eyelet row: (WS) P4, (p2tog, yrn, p9) 5 times, p2tog, yrn, p4.
Beg with a knit row work 100 rows in st st.
Place a marker at each end of the last row.
Work a further 20 rows.
Work in pattern from chart.
Row 1: K11A, pattern across 44 sts of row 1 of chart, k10A.
Row 2: P10A, pattern across 44 sts of row 2 of chart, p11A.
Continue working in st st foll chart, until 60 rows of chart have been completed.
Work 19 rows in A in st st.
Eyelet row: (WS) P4, (p2tog, yrn, p9) 5 times, p2tog, yrn, p4.
Change to 4mm needles.
Knit 11 rows.
Cast off.

FINISHING OFF
Join side seams, noting that coloured threads form the fold line. Cut six pieces of yarn approximately 59in (150cm) long. Make a plait and thread through eyelets to form a tie. Cut 3 x 39in (1m) lengths of rope, and form a plait. Sew at inside top to form a handle.

ALTERNATIVES
Use the Jolly Roger motif to make a cushion cover, a throw or a fun wall hanging on a flagpole.

TOY BAG CHART
(44 sts x 60 rows)

44 sts

Key to chart

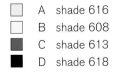

A   shade 616
B   shade 608
C   shade 613
D   shade 618

1 square represents 1 stitch and 1 row

Nursery Organizer

Soft chunky yarn in double moss stitch is used for the base
of the container, with baby merino DK for the clock face.
This project is not just for practical storage – the
clock can also be detached and played with.

MATERIALS
- Garnstudio Eskimo, 100% wool
  (54yd/49m per 50g ball):
  7 balls in shade 01 Off White (A)
- Garnstudio Baby Merino DK,
  100% wool (191yd/175m per
  50g ball):
  1 ball each of: shade 02 Off White
  (B), shade 22 Light Grey (C),
  shade 09 Lime (D), shade 10
  Light Turquoise (E), shade 04
  Yellow (F)
- Small amount of red and dark
  brown yarn for embroidery
- 5.5mm (US9:UK5) and 6mm
  (US10:UK4) circular needle
- A pair each of 3.75mm (US5:UK9)
  and 6mm (US10:UK4) needles
- 2 x 3.75mm (US5:UK9) double-
  pointed needles
- Toy stuffing
- Hook-and-loop fastening tape

FINISHED SIZE
12in (30cm) diameter, 8in (20cm)
deep

TENSION
Container: 13 sts and 20 rows
to 4in (10cm) over pattern using
6mm needles
Clock: 24 sts and 32 rows to
4in (10cm) over st st using
3.75mm needles

CONTAINER

With 6mm needles and A, cast on 5 sts.

Next row: Inc in each of next 2 sts, k1, inc in each of next 2 sts (9 sts).

Row 1 and every foll alt row: P to end.

Row 2: (K1, m1) to last st, k1 (17 sts).

Row 4: (K2, m1) to last st, k1 (25 sts).

Row 6: (K3, m1) to last st, k1 (33 sts).

Cont in this way, increasing 8 sts on 12 foll RS rows (129 sts).

Row 31: P to end.

Change to 6mm circular needle and use yarn double.

Mark the end of this row with a coloured thread for the end of the base.

Cont in rounds to form sides.

Next round: K3, (k2tog, k4) to end (108 sts).

Next round: P to end to form edge of base.

Next round: K to end.

Next round: P to end.

Working in double moss st, cont as follows:

Rounds 1 and 2: (K1, p1) to end.

Rounds 3 and 4: (P1, k1) to end.

These 4 rounds form the double moss st and are repeated throughout.

Continue straight until work measures 6in (15cm) from marker.

Change to 5.5mm circular needle.

Next round: P to end.

Next round: K to end.

Next round: P to end.

Cast off knitwise.

With WS facing, gather around cast-on edge and pull up tightly.

Join base seam.

CLOCK
Front

With 3.75mm needles and B, cast on 5 sts.

Next row: Inc in each of next 2 sts, k1, inc in each of next 2 sts (9 sts).

Row 1 and every foll alt row: P to end.

Row 2: (K1, m1) to last st, k1 (17 sts).

Row 4: (K2, m1) to last st, k1 (25 sts).

Row 6: (K3, m1) to last st, k1 (33 sts).

Cont in this way, increasing 8 sts on 6 foll RS rows (81 sts).

Row 20: P to end.

Break off B.

Join in E.

Cont in this way, increasing 8 sts on 4 foll RS rows (113 sts).

Purl 2 rows.

Next row: (K14, m1) to last st, k1 (121 sts).

Back

Purl 2 rows.

Next row: (K13, skpo) to last st, k1 (113 sts).

Next row and every foll alt row: P to end.

Next row: (K12, skpo) to last st, k1 (105 sts).

Cont in this way, decreasing 8 sts on 3 foll RS rows (81 sts).

Break off E.

Join in B.

Purl 1 row.

Next row: (K8, skpo) to last st, k1 (73 sts).

Next row and every foll alt row: P to end.

Cont in this way, decreasing 8 sts on 8 foll RS rows (9 sts).

Purl 1 row.

Next row: (K2tog) twice, k1, (k2tog) twice (5 sts).

Finishing the clock

Break off yarn and thread through sts. Fasten off tightly and join row ends, stuffing lightly as you go. Run gathering thread round cast-on sts, pull up tightly and fasten off. Using red embroidery thread, embroider French knots (see page 45) around face of clock and one in D at centre of clock. Embroider hands using chain stitch and E. Embroider top of hands in red and satin stitch.

SMALL PENDULUM DISCS
(make 2)

With 3.75mm needles and F, cast on 5 sts.

Next row: Inc in each of next 2 sts, k1, inc in each of next 2 sts (9 sts).

Row 1 and every foll alt row: P to end.

Row 2: (K1, m1) to last st, k1 (17 sts).

Row 4: (K2, m1) to last st, k1 (25 sts).

Row 6: (K3, m1) to last st, k1 (33 sts).

Purl 3 rows.

Next row: (K2, skpo) to last st, k1 (25 sts).

Next and every foll alt row: P to end.

Next row: (K1, skpo) to last st, k1 (17 sts).

Next row: (Skpo) to last st, k1 (9 sts).

Next row: (K2tog) twice, k1, (k2tog) twice (5 sts).

Finishing the small pendulums

Break off yarn and thread through sts. Fasten off tightly and join row ends, stuffing lightly as you go. Run gathering thread round cast-on sts, pull up tightly and fasten off.

LARGE PENDULUM DISC HANDLES
(make 2)

Using 3.75mm needles and F, cast on 5 sts.

Next row: Inc in each of next 2 sts, k1, inc in each of next 2 sts (9 sts).

Row 1 and every foll alt row: P to end.

Row 2: (K1, m1) to last st, k1 (17 sts).

Row 4: (K2, m1) to last st, k1 (25 sts).

Cont in this way, increasing 8 sts on 3 foll RS rows (49 sts).

Purl 3 rows.

Next row: (K4, skpo) to last st, k1 (41) sts.

Next and every foll alt row: P to end.

Next row: (K3, skpo) to last st, k1 (33) sts.

Cont in this way, decreasing 8 sts on 3 foll RS rows (9 sts).

Purl 1 row.

Next row: (K2tog) twice, k1, (k2tog) twice (5 sts).

Finishing the large pendulum

Break off yarn and thread through sts. Fasten off tightly and join row ends, stuffing lightly as you go. Run gathering thread round cast-on sts, pull up tightly and fasten off.

CORDS
(make 1 each of the following lengths: 7in/18cm, 6in/15cm and 5in/12cm)

Using 3.75mm double-pointed needles and D, cast on 4 sts.

Row 1: K to end, do not turn work.

Row 2: Slip sts to the other end of the needle, take yarn across back of work, pull tightly, k4, do not turn work.

Rep row 2 until cord is required length.

Next row: (K2tog) twice.

Next row: K2tog.

Fasten off.

FINISHING OFF

Sew large disc handles onto the top of the container, opposite each other and with half of the disc showing above the top. Sew the mouse and two smaller discs to end of cords. Sew small pieces of hook-and-loop fastening tape to the back of the clock and container so that the clock can be removed.

MOUSE
(starting at back)

With 3.75mm needles and C, cast on 6 sts.

Purl 1 row.

Next row: Inc in every st (12 sts).

Work in st st for 3 rows.

Next row: (K1, m1) to last st, k1 (23 sts).

Work in st st for 5 rows.

Next row: (K3, k2tog) 4 times, k3 (19 sts).

Next and every foll alt row: P to end.

Next row: (K2, k2tog) 4 times, k3 (15 sts).

Next row: (K1, k2tog) to end (10 sts).

Next row: (K2tog) to end (5 sts).

Next row: K2tog, k1, k2tog (3 sts).

Break off yarn and thread through sts. Join row ends. Make a twisted cord for tail.

Ears (make 2)

With 3.75mm needles and C, cast on 6 sts.

Purl 1 row.

Next row: (K2tog) 3 times.

Break off yarn and thread through sts.

Fasten off.

Finishing the mouse

Sew cast-off edges of mouse body together from back to front, stuffing firmly as you go. Attach ears and a tail made from a twisted cord. Embroider eyes using French knots (see page 45) in a dark brown yarn.

Draught Excluder

Organic wool in cool neutrals is used for this
simple-to-knit pebble draught excluder.
As well as helping to keep a room warm,
it also introduces a fun coastal theme.

MATERIALS
- Rico Organic Pure Chunky, 100%
  wool (87yd/80m per 50g ball)
  1 ball each of:
  shade 001 Off White (A)
  shade 002 Beige (B)
  shade 004 Light Grey (C)
- A pair of 5.5mm (US9:UK5)
  needles
- Stuffing

FINISHED SIZES
Large pebble: 6in (15cm) long,
3½in (9cm) high
Medium pebble: 5in (12.5cm)
long, 3in (7cm) high
Small pebble: 4in (10cm) long, 2in
(5cm) high
To fit average doorway: 31in
(80cm). Seven pebbles made

TENSION
14 sts and 19 rows to 4in (10cm)
over st st using 5.5mm needles

LARGE PEBBLE
(make 1 in B)

Using 5.5mm needles, cast on 3 sts.

Row 1: Inc knitwise in every st (6 sts).

Row 2 and every foll alternate row:
P to end.

Row 3: Inc knitwise in every st (12 sts).

Row 5: (K1, inc in next st) to end (18 sts).

Row 7: (K2, inc in next st) to end
(24 sts) **.

Cont increasing in this way to 42 sts.

Starting with a purl row, work 9 rows st st.

Row 23: (K5, k2tog) to end (36 sts).

Row 24 and every foll alternate row:
P to end.

Row 25: (K4, k2tog) to end (30 sts).

Continue decreasing in this way to 12 sts,
ending with a purl row.

Next row: (K2tog) to end (6 sts).

Cast off.

ALTERNATIVES
This draught excluder can be
made to any length. Or, a few
loose pebbles in a bowl would
make an unusual decorative
feature for a hallway or room.

MEDIUM PEBBLE
(make 3 in C, 1 in A and 1 in B)

Work as given for large pebble to **.

Cont increasing in this way to 36 sts.

Starting with a purl row, work 7 rows st st.

Row 19: (K4 sts, k2tog) to end
(30 sts).

Row 20 and every foll alternate row:
P to end.

Row 21: (K3, k2tog) to end (24 sts).

Cont decreasing in this way to 12 sts,
ending with a purl row.

Next row: K2tog to end (6 sts).

Cast off.

SMALL PEBBLE
(make 1 in A)

Cast on 10 sts.

Beg with a k row, work 2 rows st st.

Row 1: (K1, inc in next st) to end (15 sts).

Row 2 and every foll alternate row:
P to end.

Row 3: (K2, inc in next st) to end (20 sts).

Row 5: (K3, inc in next st) to end (25 sts).

Starting with a purl row, st st for 9 rows.

Row 15: (K3, k2tog) to end (20 sts).

Row 16 and every foll alternate row:
P to end.

Row 17: (K2, k2tog) to end (15 sts).

Row 19: (K1, k2tog) to end (10 sts).

Starting with a purl row, work 3 rows st st.

Cast off.

FINISHING OFF

Leaving a gap for stuffing, sew up seam of
each pebble. Stuff firmly. Tack together at
the ends to form a line, pulling pebbles
close together.

Getting Started

ALTERNATIVES

For each project, there are suggestions for other ways to use the pattern to create alternative items. A more individual result can be achieved by changing colour combinations or yarns, too.

YARN SUBSTITUTION

Choosing a yarn is part of the pleasure of knitting and crochet. Substituting a yarn will make the project more personal but there are a couple of points to remember. If you change yarns, make sure that the substitute one is the same weight as the original, and also knits to the same tension, as a different one will change the finished size of the item. Check the ball band for yardage, too, as any difference may mean that you need more or fewer balls of yarn. Bear in mind the function of the item you are making. For example, for projects for a baby, a really soft, smooth yarn is important. For rooms such as the bathroom, cotton works better than wool because it is easily washable.

TENSION SWATCHES

Making a tension swatch is a good idea before starting any project, to see if you need to change needle sizes to achieve the correct tension. If you are substituting yarn, it will also help to give you an idea of how the finished project will look.

READING PATTERNS

Before starting to knit, read through the pattern carefully. Check the abbreviations that the pattern uses, especially ones that you are less familiar with.

FOLLOWING CHARTS

There are a few colourwork charts in the booklet. As with all knitting charts, one square represents one stitch, and a row of squares a row of knitting. On a RS row follow the chart from right to left, and on a WS row begin from left to right. Knitting starts in the bottom right-hand corner. Refer to the colour key for which colours to use. Using a chart ruler is a good idea or, alternatively, photocopy the chart and mark off each row as you knit it.

Knitting Techniques

CASTING ON

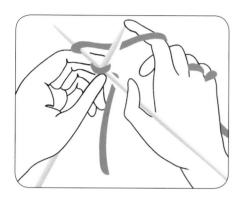

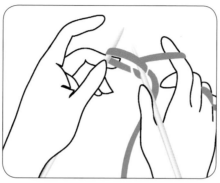

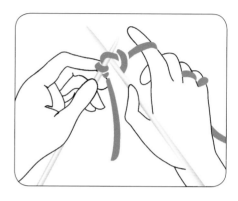

1 Make a loop on the left-hand needle, and secure with a slip knot. Holding the needle with the loop in your left hand, take the right-hand needle and insert it through the loop from front to back. Wrap the yarn around the right-hand needle.

2 Draw the yarn under and through to create a new loop. Slip this onto the left-hand needle.

3 Repeat until you have the correct number of stitches for the pattern.

CASTING OFF

1 Work the first two stitches of the cast-off row, pass the first stitch over the top of the second stitch and off the needle.

2 Repeat until one stitch remains. Cut yarn and thread through the last stitch and pull to secure.

KNIT STITCH (K)

1 After cast-on row, hold the needle with cast-on stitches in the left hand. Insert the right-hand needle into the first stitch and wrap yarn around, with the yarn held at back of the work.

2 Pull yarn through, creating a new loop.

3 Slip the new stitch onto the right-hand needle. Continue to end of row.

PURL STITCH (P)

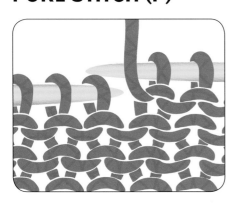

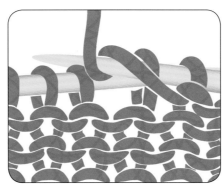

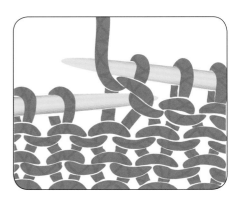

1 Hold the yarn at the front of the work.

2 Place the right-hand needle into the first stitch from front to back. Wrap the yarn around the right-hand needle anti-clockwise.

3 Bring the needle back through the stitch and pull through.

OTHER STITCHES

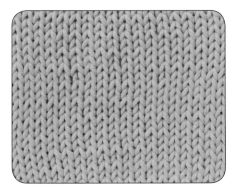

STOCKING STITCH
K on RS rows, P on WS rows.

REVERSE STOCKING STITCH
K on WS rows, P on RS rows.

MOSS STITCH
Worked on an even number of stitches.
Row 1: (K1, p1) to end.
Row 2: (P1, k1) to end.
Repeat these two rows.

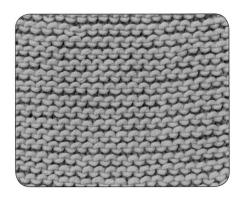

GARTER STITCH
K on every row.

CABLES

Using a cable needle, cables are formed over varied numbers of stitches by crossing one set of stitches over another.

BASIC 4-STITCH CABLE (C4F)

Worked on reverse stocking stitch.

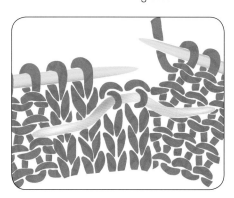

1 Slip next 2 sts onto a cable needle and hold at front of work.

2 Knit the next 2 sts from the left-hand needle, then K2 from the cable needle.

The same cable can be worked as C4B, holding the stitches on the cable needle at the back of the work instead of the front.

INTARSIA

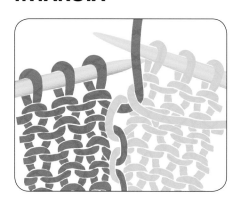

This method is used for larger areas of colourwork than Fair Isle, where the yarn is not taken across the back of the work. Separate balls of yarn are used, or smaller amounts wound onto bobbins. When a new colour is introduced into a row, twist the two yarns together at the back of the work. After knitting, press according to the yarn band instructions to neaten the join.

FELTING

After knitting and sewing up, put the item that is to be felted into a pillowcase and sew up the top. Put into a washing machine set at 140°F (60°C). Wash, but do not tumble dry. Pull into shape, putting objects into containers to help with shaping, and leave to dry.

Finishing Touches

FRENCH KNOTS

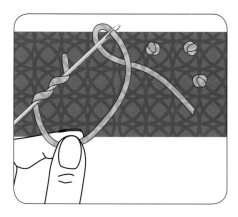

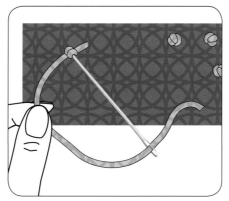

1 Bring needle from back to front of work to the point you want to place the knot. Twist yarn around needle a few times, depending on the size of knot required.

2 Insert needle back into the work, keeping yarn wrapped around needle tightly. Feed the yarn through the twists just made. Secure at the back of the work.

CHAIN STITCH

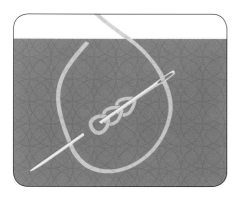

Make a knot to secure yarn at the back of the work. Bring the needle to the front. Insert the needle near the starting point, and bring it out again a short distance away, leaving it in the fabric. Wrap the yarn underneath needle. Pull the needle out to form a chain. Repeat as required.

SATIN STITCH

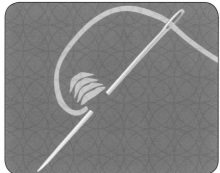

Make a knot to secure yarn at the back of the work. Bring the needle to front of work. Insert needle from front to back, forming a stitch the length required. Repeat until there are enough stitches for the motif you are doing.

Sewing Up

MATTRESS STITCH

Use mattress stitch for an invisible seam and a neat finish. After pressing, place the pieces side by side with RS facing. Starting at the bottom, secure the yarn and bring the needle up between the first and second stitch on one piece. Find the corresponding point on the other piece, and insert the needle there. Keep the sewing-up yarn loose as you work up the seam, then pull tight.

BACKSTITCH

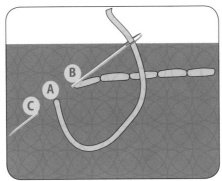

Make a knot to secure yarn at back of the work. Bring the needle up at point **A**, insert at point **B** and bring back up at point **C**. Repeat, keeping the stitches at an even length.

Abbreviations

beg	beginning
C4[6]B	cable 4[6] back: slip next 2[3] sts onto a cable needle and hold at back of work, k2[3], then k2[3] from cable needle
C4[6]F	cable 4[6] front: slip next 2[3] sts onto a cable needle and hold at front of work, k2[3], then k2[3] from cable needle
cont	continue
Cr2L	cross 2 left: slip next st onto a cable needle and leave at front of work, k1, then k1 from cable needle
Cr2Lp	cross 2 left purlwise: slip next st onto a cable needle and leave at front of work, p1, then k1 from cable needle.
Cr2R	cross 2 right: slip next st on cable needle and leave at back of work, k1, then k1 from cable needle
Cr2Rp	cross 2 right purlwise: slip next st on a cable needle and leave at back of work, k1, then p1 from cable needle.
Cr3L	cross 3 left: slip next 2 sts onto cable needle and hold at front of work, p1, then k2 from cable needle
Cr3R	cross 3 right: slip next st onto cable needle and hold at back of work, k2, then p1 from cable needle
Cr4L	cross 4 left: slip next 3 sts onto cable needle and hold at front of work, p1, then k3 from cable needle
Cr4R	cross 4 right: slip next st onto cable needle and hold at back of work, k3, then p1 from cable needle
Cr5L	cross 5 left: slip next 3 sts onto cable needle and hold at front of work, p2, then k3 from cable needle
Cr5R	cross 5 right: slip next 2 sts onto cable needle and hold at back of work, k3, then p2 from cable needle
dec	decrease
foll	following
g st	garter stitch, every row knit
inc	increase by working twice into stitch
k	knit
k2tog	knit two stitches together
m1	make 1 st by picking up the bar between the st just worked and the next st on LH needle then k into back of it
MB	make bobble: k into front, back, front and back of next st, (turn, p4, turn, k4) twice, then pass 2nd, 3rd and 4th sts over the first to complete the bobble
MK	make knot: (k1, p1, k1, p1, k1, p1) all in next st, pass 2nd, 3rd, 4th, 5th and 6th sts over the first to complete the knot
p	purl
p2tog	purl 2 sts together
p3tog	purl 3 sts together
psso	pass slipped st over
rem	remaining
rep	repeat
rev st st	reverse stocking stitch: p on right side and k on wrong side
RS	right side of work
skpo	sl1, k1, then pass slipped stitch over
sl	slip
ss	slip stitch
st(s)	stitch(es)
st st	stocking stitch, k on RS and p on WS
tbl	through the back of the loop
tog	together
TW2l	twist 2 left: k into back of 2nd st on left needle, then into front of first st and slip both sts off the needle together
WS	wrong side of work
yf	yarn forward
yrh	yarn round hook
yrn	yarn round needle to make a stitch
( )	repeat instructions inside brackets

Conversions

NEEDLE SIZES

UK	Metric	US
14	2mm	0
13	2.5mm	1
12	2.75mm	2
11	3mm	–
10	3.25mm	3
–	3.5mm	4
9	3.75mm	5
8	4mm	6
7	4.5mm	7
6	5mm	8
5	5.5mm	9
4	6mm	10
3	6.5mm	10.5
2	7mm	10.5
1	7.5mm	11
0	8mm	11
00	9mm	13
000	10mm	15

UK/US YARN WEIGHTS

UK	US
2-ply	Lace
3-ply	Fingering
4-ply	Sport
Double knitting (DK)	Light worsted
Aran	Fisherman/worsted
Chunky	Bulky
Super chunky	Extra bulky